S. Shakthidharan is a western Sydney storyteller with Sri Lankan heritage and Tamil ancestry. He's a writer, director and producer of theatre and film, and composer of original music. Belvoir: *The Jungle and the Sea* (co-written with Eamon Flack) and *Counting and Cracking* (associate writer Eamon Flack). He has in development a new play with Belvoir and a co-commission with the Melbourne Theatre Company and Sydney Theatre Company. He has a feature film with Felix Media and a new TV project also in development. Shakthi's memoir *Gather Up Your World In One Long Breath* comes out in September 2025 with Powerhouse Publishing. His debut play *Counting and Cracking* received critical, commercial and community acclaim. The script won the Victorian Premier's Literature Prize and the NSW Premier's Nick Enright Prize for Playwriting; the production won seven Helpmann and three Sydney Theatre Awards. Shakthi's most recent play *The Jungle and the Sea*, again was met with rave reviews and had a profound impact on the Sri Lankan community. It won the 2024 Victorian Premier's Drama Prize and four Sydney Theatre Awards including Best Mainstage Production. Shakthi is the Director of Kurinji, was previously Director of Co-Curious, and was Founder and Artistic Director of CuriousWorks from 2003-2018. He is a Creative Australia and Sidney Myer Fellow, and a recipient of the Philip Parsons and Kirk Robson awards.

Radhika Mudaliyar, Nadie Kammallaweera, Vaishnavi Suryaprakash and Manali Datar in rehearsal (Photo: Brett Boardman)

Manali Datar in rehearsal (Photo: Brett Boardman)

THE WRONG GODS

BY S.SHAKTHIDHARAN

CURRENT THEATRE SERIES

First published in 2025
by Currency Press Pty Ltd,
Gadigal Land, Suite 310, 46–56 Kippax Street, Surry Hills, NSW 2010, Australia
enquiries@currency.com.au
www.currency.com.au

in association with Belvoir

Typeset by Brighton Gray for Currency Press.
Cover image shows Radhika Mudaliyar and Nadie Kammallaweera; cover design by Alphabet Studios; photo by Daniel Boud.

Currency Press acknowledges the Traditional Owners of the Country on which we live and work. We pay our respects to all Aboriginal and Torres Strait Islander Elders, past and present.

Contents

Writer's Note *vii*

THE WRONG GODS 1

Hannah Goodwin in rehearsal (Photo: Brett Boardman)

S. Shakthidharan and Radhika Mudaliyar in rehearsal (Photo: Brett Boardman)

Writer's note

She's sitting on the banks of her river, deep in her valley, in the remote heart of India. She's staring at me. I'm brushing off her soil from my lenses, my tripod, my cables. I've just finished an interview with her. As I head back up the mountain, to where my Australian arts colleagues are waiting, she yells: 'Make sure you get our story onto that TV!' It's not a request: it's an order. Her cow bellows his support. 'I'll try, aunty,' I feebly call back down the mountain.

Some twelve years later, I can still feel the force of her words. Partly because of the shame of being a lowly theatre maker, and not a famous TV presenter that can give her story the cultural power (although probably not the nuance) it deserves. But more so, because of the sophistication of her thinking. She has come to learn, in the most brutal way possible, that the fate of her home is intimately tied up with separate events happening elsewhere in her country, and indeed all over the world. She has learnt that she must now understand the power of some new gods, gods that have never entered her valley or felt her river before. But she is not facing this challenge with fear. She and her fellow community members have summoned the strength to face these new gods head on.

What will it take for us city folk to go through the same process? To question our own gods, and be prepared to meet new (or old) ones? We believe we have broken from the shackles of communal life and can be our full individual selves—but has there ever been a time in the history of our earth more culturally homogenous than now? We think we have become more secular, more accepting of multiple faiths—but has there ever been a religion humanity has more quickly and wholly accepted than the religion of progress?

We will soon be forced to grapple with the consequences of our most deeply held faiths, whether we like it or not. It might be in the wake of the next natural disaster, fascist leader or disruptive technology, or in some strange mix of all three. But it will come.

How will we gather the acuity to deal with what's heading towards us? How do we use the coming crises as opportunities for real change?

Certainly, we will need to first appreciate how much power we all wield in the modern world, with every decision we make—financial, social, political, cultural. And we will need to seriously consider that maybe we are giving that power to the wrong people. We are putting our faith in the wrong ideas. The wrong systems. The wrong gods.

That woman, in the valley. Her gods and our gods are going to need to talk to each other. They are going to have to work together. It will take an openness on both sides. They are ready. But are we?

Nadie Kammallaweera in rehearsal (Photo: Brett Boardman)

Vaishnavi Suryaprakash and Radhika Mudaliyar in rehearsal (Photo: Brett Boardman)

The Wrong Gods was first produced by Belvoir St Theatre with Melbourne Theatre Company, at Belvoir St Theatre, Gadigal Country, Sydney, on 3 May 2025, with the following cast:

DEVI	Manali Datar
NIRMALA	Nadie Kammallaweera
ISHA	Radhika Mudaliyar
LAKSHMI	Vaishnavi Suryaprakash

Writer and Co-Director, S. Shakthidharan
Co-Director, Hannah Goodwin
Set and Costume Designer, Keerthi Subramanyam
Lighting Designer, Amelia Lever-Davidson
Sound Designer, Steve Francis
Associate Sound Designer, Madeleine Picard
Composer, Sabyasachi (Rahul) Bhattacharya
Movement and Fight Director, Intimacy Coordinator, Nigel Poulton
Vocal Coach, Laura Farrell

CHARACTERS

NIRMALA. South Asian appearance, fifties.
ISHA. South Asian appearance, twenties.
LAKSHMI. South Asian appearance, forties.
DEVI. South Asian appearance, thirties.

SETTING

A riverbank in the Narmada Valley, India.

LANGUAGE

Didi – older sister (also a term of respect to an elder).
Maa – mother.
Baba – father.

NOTE

A forward slash (/) in the dialogue indicates that the next line should start being read at this moment. The previous line is still read to its conclusion; there is simply an overlap between the two.

This playtext went to press before the end of rehearsals and may differ from the play as performed.

ACT ONE

We are deep in the heart of India. In a small clearing, at the base of a valley, between two mountain ranges. Along the bottom of the valley runs a river.

In the clearing are recently harvested vegetables, water and milk vessels, traditional agricultural tools.

NIRMALA *and* ISHA *enter, carrying coconuts and oil lamps to the riverbank, preparing for a simple ceremony. They are mid-argument:*

ISHA: School doesn't go all year, Maa, it has breaks—

NIRMALA: That school has breaks when those city people want to have breaks. How is that supposed to work with us? / We are in the middle of harvest, Isha!

ISHA: I can do all the work you need me to do here and still do / all the work I want to do there—

NIRMALA: Don't be stupid. You are not some mountain goat, built to spend your days travelling—

ISHA: I will find a way to make it all work. / Let me try at least!

NIRMALA: Nonsense. You can't. That school is too far away.

ISHA: [*petulant*] Yes—and that's exactly what I like about it!

NIRMALA: You have everything you need here!

ISHA: Nothing ever changes here!

NIRMALA: Oh, the river never moves, is that it? The trees do not grow? / The clouds stay still? The animals are frozen, are they Isha?

ISHA: You! I—Argh! You're always right, aren't you?

NIRMALA: Yes. I suppose I am. What to do?

ISHA: What is the point of even talking to you / if you never actually listen—

NIRMALA: What *is* the point, when you are so stubborn—

ISHA: Who do you think I learnt it from? / Huh? Maa?

NIRMALA: / You—I—ARGH!

ISHA: ARGH!

Beat.

NIRMALA: Put the items down there.

ISHA: Okay.

ISHA *dutifully puts the items down.* NIRMALA *starts arranging them for the ceremony.* ISHA *wanders over to her Bommai Kolu: a collection of female religious figurines assembled on a rocky ledge.*

NIRMALA: I don't have time for all this, Isha. Not today. We have the harvest, and the feast, and we need to pray, to gather strength, to, to—

ISHA *is examining the idols; not listening to her mother.*

Isha!

ISHA: Mmm?

NIRMALA *is about to yell at her, but then lets it go; she watches her daughter, concerned.*

NIRMALA: You are spending too much time with those idols.

ISHA: They are just another version of our gods.

NIRMALA: Our gods have been through more than these have. They have better stories to tell.

ISHA: Miss Devi gave me these. / They were a gift from her—

NIRMALA: 'Miss Devi' this, 'Miss Devi' that. I regret introducing you to bloody Miss Devi.

ISHA: Don't worry, Maa. I'm just curious. / That's all.

NIRMALA: You're curious about everything in the bloody universe—

ISHA: Who had the courage to do that? To change a god? Why weren't they happy with ours? Why did they have to put human faces on them?

NIRMALA: This is why Miss Devi loved you so much, no? Because you would ask her crazy questions like this.

ISHA: She too asks the same kind of questions. We used to find out the answers together.

NIRMALA: When you were at that school, you should have told that Miss Devi: We see our gods in our water and our trees. They embrace us, always. We do not need her idols.

ISHA: Well, you could let me go back to school, / and then I could tell her—

NIRMALA: Isha. You know how hard it was to get you into that place? I had to track down that bloody Miss Devi, she only convinced that headteacher to get you that scholarship, she only let you stay with her in her own home / during school term—

ISHA: I know, Maa, I know—

NIRMALA: You think I wanted to pull you out? After everything I did for you to get you in there?

ISHA: No. / Sorry, Maa—

NIRMALA: Things have changed now, no? With your father—/ And I—

ISHA: [*softer*] I know, Maa. I know you need me here now. And here I am.

NIRMALA: Hm. Anyway. I can teach you much more than that silly Miss Devi can. Does she know the eighty-four different types of fruit you can pick in this forest?

ISHA: No.

NIRMALA: No. She would probably die trying to pick fruit in this forest. Stupid Miss Devi. Does she know how to plant cucumber and gourd in the bottom of this valley after the tide has gone back, and millets, grains and beans higher up on the mountains when the tide is in?

ISHA: No, Maa.

NIRMALA: No. Useless Miss Devi. Does she know how to tell when the river will come closer to us, and when it will go away, before the river has even done so? Without beakers or batteries or god knows whatever other gadgets they had you using, but by being able to just listen to the river, listen only with her eyes and her ears and heart?

ISHA: No, Maa. She doesn't.

NIRMALA: No. She doesn't know any of these things. But I do. *We* do, Isha. No-one else knows those things about this part of the world. But we do. / That is something, no?

But ISHA *is distracted, she's spied something unusual behind her Kolu.*

ISHA: Maa! Look!

NIRMALA: Oh, child. Will you ever listen to me?

ISHA: Look!

NIRMALA: What, Isha?!

ISHA: Eggs.

NIRMALA: [*surprised*] Eggs?

NIRMALA *walks over.*

NIRMALA: Hm.

ISHA: What?

NIRMALA: Your idols. They have made good protection from the wind. Clever birds. Maybe it is the *dongar?*

ISHA: The owls?

NIRMALA: Mmm. Duda!

ISHA: Do you think it's the *dongar duda?* The forest owlet?

NIRMALA: Maybe.

ISHA: '*Athene blewitti.*'

NIRMALA: What?

ISHA: That is what scientists call them. At school. It's their proper name. / Miss Devi taught us—

NIRMALA: Their 'proper name'? What language was that?

ISHA: Latin.

NIRMALA: What?

ISHA: It's a language from Europe.

NIRMALA: Where do they speak it?

ISHA: They don't speak it anymore.

NIRMALA: Why does that school force you to use a language that no-one uses anymore to describe the bird?

ISHA: Because that's what scientists everywhere use. So we all know the same name.

NIRMALA: Who invented this crazy system?

ISHA: A dead white man from Europe. / Maa, listen—

NIRMALA: So everyone must now use it?

ISHA: He did it first, I guess. / Maa, can we—

NIRMALA: Are you saying he knew this bird before we did?

ISHA: Maa! Can we take the eggs back with us?

NIRMALA: What?

ISHA: If we leave them here, they'll get eaten. By the crows; that damn cobra—

NIRMALA: If we take them, what will the mother bird do? Or the father bird? Huh? When they come back, and find their children are gone?

ISHA: But if it's the forest owlet it's endangered. Critically endangered!

NIRMALA: Isha. The birds, the animals. The river, the mountain, the sky. They have their *own* system. They have kept things in balance for far longer than humans have even existed. Why do you always think you know better? Why must you get involved?

ISHA: Maybe we just take one.

NIRMALA: No.

ISHA: Maybe I can take it into school one day, for a little visit, and they can study it. One of the days we have to visit town anyway. I'll just slip into school / for a second—

NIRMALA: No!

ISHA: But, Maa!

NIRMALA: Leave it, Isha! There is knowledge also in leaving something alone, no? In looking at something exactly where it belongs. / Will you ever understand this?

ISHA: Just / one egg—

NIRMALA: Shut up! Idiot child. Come. It is time to talk to *our* gods.

NIRMALA *faces the river with respect.* ISHA *does the same; she's been doing this since she was a toddler.*

Mighty river. You were born out of injustice. You began life as a little girl. The man you were supposed to marry betrayed you. But you did not shrink. No. You became immense. You charged furiously through this land, shattering rocks, forming valleys, reaching caves at the tops of mountains and burrowing deep underground, knowing where the roots of our great trees would one day grow. No-one could stop you. Through your fury, life became possible. You became a god. You kicked the man who betrayed you with such force he was thrown back to where he came from, carried on the wind. He thought he was some kind of king; invincible. But he was a demon. Only a woman could bring an end to him.

NIRMALA *picks up a scythe and cleaves the largest of the pumpkins in two. She smears red kumkum powder (turmeric and lime) over the inside of the vegetable.*

Goddess. We need your power today. For a new demon is coming to our village. *Money*. Oh river, I need you to rise now and drive those rich American bastards out of our valley for good. And if they don't leave—if they refuse to—cut off their heads, will you? Or even just their—

She mimes the act of having testicles.

—balls will do.

ISHA: [*laughing*] Maa!

NIRMALA: My husband is just a man. But we are *you.* Give us your strength, and we will do this. We will drive that demon out.

They make signs to ward off the evil eye.

ISHA: They're coming? Today?

NIRMALA *looks out into the distance.*

NIRMALA: So I've been told.

ISHA: [*to herself*] They're coming. Today.

ISHA *looks into the distance now.*

Huh.

NIRMALA: It has to stop with us. If we stop them, we spare everyone else the pain. Yes, Isha? Isha?

ISHA *is lost in her own thoughts.*

Isha! Are you listening to me, child?

ISHA: [*not listening*] Yes, Maa.

NIRMALA *walks away from the river, to the edge of her field.*

NIRMALA: [*serious*] Isha. Look.

ISHA *follows her mother.* NIRMALA *gestures offstage.* ISHA *looks in the direction she is pointing.*

Remember?

ISHA: The caves?

NIRMALA: Isha—

ISHA: I remember, Maa. The paintings.

NIRMALA: Yes. The paintings. Of our way of life; in the forests, in the river. You convinced me, once, to get some fellow in from the city. To test those rocks, with their gadgets. See how old the drawings were.

ISHA: They said it was at least fifty thousand years.

NIRMALA: What they painted, fifty thousand years ago, we are still doing now, no?

ISHA: The battle scenes were my favourite.

NIRMALA: When you were little, you would crawl in there and sit and stare at them for hours.

ISHA: I remember.

NIRMALA: You'd stare at the chieftains and kings and queens and soldiers and missionaries and every other person that has come in here with their big plans for us. Always trying to come in here and change us. Fifty thousand years they've been trying, Isha. And have they ever won?

ISHA: No. They have never won.

NIRMALA: That's right. Our village—led by *our* family line—has always kept them out. It is our ancestral duty, Isha, to resist. To stop the latest demon. It is a role our family has always played. And now we must continue to play it. Do you understand what I am saying?

ISHA: [*overwhelmed, dutiful*] Yes, Maa.

NIRMALA *picks up some vegetables.*

NIRMALA: Good. Come. We have a harvest, no?! We have worked hard. And tonight, we celebrate. We feast. Gather some black pepper, cardamom, cinnamon and curcuma from the edge of the forest. Then come to the fire. The other families will be coming tonight, we need to finish cooking.

ISHA *is staring off into the distance.*

And don't dawdle, okay? Or I will break your backside in two / I swear to all the gods in the bloody universe—

ISHA: Okay, Maa! Got it! Stop shouting at me!

NIRMALA *exits, swearing about her daydreaming daughter as she goes.* ISHA *makes sure her mother has gone, then looks at the river, then the Kolu. She closes her eyes, and prays.*

Goddesses? *Any* of you. I have a *tiiiiiiiny* favour to ask. When you drive those foreigners out of our little village, can you … let them take me, too?

LAKSHMI *enters, quietly.* ISHA *oblivious to her entrance; continues to pray.*

If I stay here, I will have to marry a man.

She grimaces.

Probably that sour-smelling Ranjan, with the chipped yellow tooth.

She grimaces again.

I will not become a scientist. I will just become … the same as Maa. Blergh! I have walked every path in these mountains. Turned every stone, stared at every cloud. There's a lot beyond this place. You let me taste a bit of that at school. And then you took it away. That's not fair, no? Anyway. There you are. Goddesses. All of you. You have heard the prayers of my mother. And I have given you my own too. As always, you will choose what's best.

Her prayer finished, ISHA *turns around—and is shocked to see a stranger.*

LAKSHMI: Hello.

ISHA*'s too stunned to reply.*

Sorry. I didn't want to disturb you, before—Are you—

ISHA *quickly gathers herself. She smiles blankly and goes to walk past* LAKSHMI.

Hey! It's okay. You don't have to be polite with me.

ISHA *continues to walk away.*

Did they tell you not to talk to me?

ISHA *exits.*

Do you always do what your mother tells you to do?

ISHA *re-enters.*

You deserve to, you know.

ISHA: Sorry?

LAKSHMI: See the world. Become a scientist. It's a reasonable request. You deserve that future.

ISHA: Oh. Thank you—

LAKSHMI: [*gesturing at the Kolu*] But they're not real, you know. Your gods. They can't help you. They can't answer your prayers.

ISHA: … I know.

LAKSHMI: [*surprised*] You do?

ISHA: I know they're not real. All gods are just another way to understand the divine.

LAKSHMI: [*smiling*] Ah! I knew there was more beneath the surface.

ISHA: I suppose with people like you, everything is on the surface, no? There is nothing below.

LAKSHMI: [*laughing*] You would actually have to talk to me to find out.

ISHA *gestures at her clothes.*

ISHA: People like you don't normally like to talk to people like me.

LAKSHMI: Oh, I don't believe in all that caste nonsense. Everyone is equal, don't you think?

ISHA: Of course. Or at least they should be.

LAKSHMI: Exactly.

ISHA: You learnt to speak our language?

LAKSHMI: [*nodding*] It's not so different to mine. It probably came from yours, who knows.

ISHA: So you took our language too? And changed it?

LAKSHMI: I don't know. But I could introduce you to people who would.

ISHA: Hm.

LAKSHMI *gestures again at the Kolu.*

LAKSHMI: So why do you pray to them? If you know they don't exist.

ISHA: … Because I believe in something bigger than myself.

LAKSHMI: Ah.

LAKSHMI *walks over to the idols.*

You know, the only thing you *can* really rely on, is yourself.

ISHA: Who are you? What is your name?

LAKSHMI: [*picking up an idol*] Katyayani. The goddess of power, no? And yet she is called 'Katyayani.' That's kind of pathetic, right?

ISHA: Where are you from? Are you one of those Americans? You don't sound like them.

LAKSHMI: Katyayana was a man.

ISHA: He worshipped her. She is the God. He was only the devotee.

LAKSHMI: And yet she is named after him.

ISHA: She has many names.

LAKSHMI: None of them her own.

ISHA: [*pointing at another idol*] Mahishasuramardini.

LAKSHMI: What?

ISHA: Mahishasuramardini. Named after the man she decapitated. That's my favourite.

LAKSHMI: Still named after a man. Still pathetic. Come on. What's the point of trying to understand the divine if this is the only path the men give you to walk towards it?

ISHA: You think too much, nameless, placeless person. The goddess is power. Turn away from her, and you are weak. Turn towards her, and you are strong.

LAKSHMI: No.

LAKSHMI *walks towards* ISHA. *She gently puts her finger on her chest.*

Turn towards *yourself.* And you are strong. That is all you need. *You,* Isha.

This is a new thought for ISHA. *She takes this in.*

ISHA: How do you know my name?
LAKSHMI: [*extending her hand*] Lakshmi.
ISHA: [*not taking it*] What?
LAKSHMI: My name is Lakshmi.
ISHA: The goddess of wealth. Typical.
LAKSHMI: And Isha is the destroyer. A goddess' name too.
ISHA: Aren't we all?
LAKSHMI: We are much more than that, Isha.
ISHA: More—than the gods?
LAKSHMI: Yes. More. Than the gods.
ISHA: You're mad.
LAKSHMI: You're lucky.
ISHA: What?
LAKSHMI: Those idols. They can't hear your prayers. But I was here. I did.
ISHA: So?
LAKSHMI: Would you like them answered? Your prayers?
ISHA: What are you on about?
LAKSHMI: … Tell me about Ranjan.
ISHA: Ranjan?
LAKSHMI: The boy. In your prayer. Tell me about him.
ISHA: Why?
LAKSHMI: Tell me, Isha. You'll see. Aren't you curious?

Beat.

ISHA: See … over there?

She points—deep into the valley. The opposite direction to the way LAKSHMI *entered.* LAKSHMI *follows* ISHA*'s gaze.*

A young man lives at the other end of this valley. His family's farm gets the least sunlight out of all of us. The smallest yield. But they are also the closest to the wild. The oldest parts of the forest. They keep it at bay. His ancestors did the initial clearings. The first fires, tens of thousands of years ago. That allowed us all to live here. They always get the first pick of the harvest.

LAKSHMI: A young man?

ISHA: Ranjan. A perfectly reasonable but quite pungent fellow who spends his days peeling cardamon, garlic and onions, and once fell onto a rock trying to escape an angry cobra, with unfortunate results.

She points to her teeth.

LAKSHMI: Okay …

ISHA: I am supposed to marry Ranjan.

LAKSHMI: Do you *want* to marry him?

ISHA: Oh, god no—

LAKSHMI: [*laughing*] Thank goodness—

ISHA *starts laughing too.*

Then you won't. You won't marry him, Isha.

ISHA: What?

LAKSHMI: If you don't want to marry him, I'll make sure you don't.

ISHA: Every three generations, the first born of the family at this end of the valley, closest to the towns, marries the first born at that end of the valley, closest to the wild.

LAKSHMI: We're no longer bound by our birth, Isha. Out there—in the rest of the world—we're judged not by who we *are*, but by what we *do*.

ISHA: You don't understand. It's a very big thing. Everyone comes to the ceremony. It goes on for days.

LAKSHMI: If you don't want to do it, you don't have to do it. It's simple.

ISHA: It's fixed. It's my destiny.

LAKSHMI: Nothing is fixed, Isha. Not anymore.

ISHA: Everything is fixed. And that is not, overall, a bad thing. It is just that there are some minor annoyances amongst the fixed-ness, that is all. And I will handle this in my own way, / thank you very much—

LAKSHMI: *You* cannot change it, I agree. But *I* can, you see. I can do things you cannot. Not yet, anyway. Not until I teach you.

ISHA: You have absolutely no idea what you are talking about, mad woman.

LAKSHMI: I understand it may look that way. But you don't yet understand me. Or yourself. Or what we are capable of.

ISHA: [*laughing*] You're an idiot, aren't you? I've been talking to a mad, blubbering idiot. [*Exiting*] I've had enough of your pointless riddles. My mother was right about you.

LAKSHMI: If I can do it. If I can stop your marriage to that boy. If I can help you get out of here and become a scientist … Will you start listening to me? Will you perhaps believe that I am not an idiot?

ISHA *pauses. She studies* LAKSHMI. *She can see that this woman is entirely serious.*

Will you, Isha? Yes or no? I need an answer.

ISHA: Okay, stranger. Deal. If you can help me go back to school and marry no man and go to college and become a scientist, I will start listening to you.

LAKSHMI: [*smiling*] Very good.

ISHA: My feeling is that you are most definitely an idiot.

NIRMALA: [*offstage*] Isha!

ISHA: Ah.

LAKSHMI: Is that your mother?

ISHA: [*nodding*] I'd be scared, if I was you.

LAKSHMI: Scared? Why?

ISHA: You'll see.

NIRMALA *enters, ready to smack* ISHA—

NIRMALA: I bloody well told you not to dawdle—

NIRMALA *sees* LAKSHMI.

Huh.

LAKSHMI: What?

NIRMALA: I didn't think the demon would look like this.

LAKSHMI: What did you expect?

NIRMALA: A pale, sweaty man. With a silly accent.

LAKSHMI: My clients do look and sound a bit like that. But they are clever enough to hire someone like me.

NIRMALA: Well. All of that is just make up. Underneath, you are the same as them. Greedy.

LAKSHMI: You call it greed. I call it ambition.

NIRMALA *picks up her scythe. She walks towards* LAKSHMI.

ISHA: [*to* LAKSHMI] I told you.

NIRMALA: Be quiet, child.

LAKSHMI: It's okay, Isha.

NIRMALA: White or brown, greed is greed and the devil is the devil. Get out of here.

LAKSHMI: The devil used to be white, yes. But then we decided we wanted some of what he was getting.

NIRMALA: And what is that?

LAKSHMI: Freedom, Aunty.

NIRMALA: Ha! We *are* free. You come to make us slaves.

LAKSHMI: What?! To whom would I make you a slave?

NIRMALA: To … What do you call it? [*Looking to* ISHA] What do they call it?

ISHA: The market.

NIRMALA: Ha! Yes. The 'market.' The way you twist up our words—

LAKSHMI: The market pays for what it buys. You, and the market. You depend on each other. I can teach you how to use it. Neither of you are slave, or master. Doesn't that sound like freedom? Real freedom, Aunty?

NIRMALA: Why have you come here? Just to annoy us? To our little village? Was all of America not enough for you?

LAKSHMI: Well, that depends on who you're asking. My *clients* have already reached the extent of what they can do in the West. They seek new frontiers. India is—a good place to start.

NIRMALA: They are not content with half the world, they want the other half now, too?

LAKSHMI: Something like that.

NIRMALA: Well, they can't have it. Not here. Not in our place. Get out. This is your last warning.

LAKSHMI: Aunty. Please. Let me help you.

NIRMALA: I never asked for your help.

LAKSHMI: But you need it.

NIRMALA: Get out!

LAKSHMI: Aunty! My clients. They're the future. You can't just tell them to go away.

NIRMALA: Watch me, demon.

She begins to raise her arm—

LAKSHMI: I am not here for them! My clients. Their money brings me here, but I am not here for them. Okay? I'm here for you, Nirmala. That's why I've come here. For *you*.

NIRMALA *lowers her scythe, wary now.*

NIRMALA: How do you know my name?

LAKSHMI: And your daughter. Isha.

She turns to her.

I'm here for her, too.

ISHA: / For *me*?

NIRMALA: For *her*?

LAKSHMI: Is greed so bad, if it is used to motivate good?

NIRMALA: What?

LAKSHMI: My clients hired me because I'm good. I do my research. I was in your area for some time before I chose you.

NIRMALA: Why?

LAKSHMI: Why did I choose you?

NIRMALA: Out with it, woman!

LAKSHMI: It's simple, really. Your village is the closest one to the towns. You're the interface, between that world—the future—and this world—the past.

NIRMALA: There is no future, no past. There's only now, devil.

LAKSHMI: You and your husband are the heads of the village council. If you change, then the rest of your village will follow. And, in time, so will the rest of the valley. That's why I chose you.

NIRMALA: Some research you did. My husband is no longer head of the council—

LAKSHMI: Technically, he is. Even if he is absent. I spoke to him.

ISHA: You found Baba?

LAKSHMI: I found your father with a group of men. On the other side of the forest.

ISHA: So he's alive.

LAKSHMI: Most days they are starving, or high on ganja, or both. If you want to call that living, then he is alive.

ISHA: Is he coming back?

LAKSHMI: ... No. I don't think so, Isha.

NIRMALA: That bastard.

LAKSHMI: Aunty. Your husband told me he'd spent so long bending down to the land, when he finally tried to stand up straight, he couldn't. I get it. What use was he to you anymore, beaten and bent over?

Silence.

My grandfather was a farmer too. He refused to stop working the land, even when it got hard. Really hard. My grandmother tried to convince him to give it up. To go to the city, like everyone else in his village was. But he was a stubborn old bastard. He refused. And my grandmother had to stay with him, to the end of their lives. Broken by the land.

More silence.

And you call yourselves free?

LAKSHMI *shifts her attention to* ISHA *now—*

And you, Isha. Your teacher—

ISHA: You spoke to Miss Devi?!

LAKSHMI: Miss Devi seems to think you are prodigiously talented.

ISHA *looks down, suddenly shy.*

NIRMALA: That woman spoke to you? Bloody traitor.

LAKSHMI: She cares a great deal about Isha. [*Looking at* ISHA] Miss Devi says you want to become a scientist. And that you could be. That you could be whatever you wanted to be, really. If you just came back to school. In the city.

NIRMALA: I need Isha on the land now.

LAKSHMI: Then why did you send her to school in the first place?

ISHA: Maa thinks we should get every opportunity a boy gets.

NIRMALA: Isha!

ISHA: That's what you said! When I was five years old, you said that girls have every right to go to school if boys do. You said you were never allowed to go to school even though you asked your father a million times, but when my father tried to stop *me*, you said he'd have to walk over your dead body first—

NIRMALA: Enough! Enough of that nonsense, Isha! That was before your father decided to abandon us. Now I need you here.

LAKSHMI: No, you don't.

NIRMALA: Excuse me?

LAKSHMI: You don't need her here. That's what I came to tell you, Nirmala.

ISHA: [*excited*] Maa—

NIRMALA: Shut up.

LAKSHMI: May I explain?

NIRMALA *considers, then nods.* ISHA *does a quiet happy dance.*

Would you put the weapon down, please?

NIRMALA *puts the scythe down, but keeps it close.*

LAKSHMI *opens the satchel she is carrying. Inside is a small bag, an envelope, a bottle and a carton. First, she gives* NIRMALA *the bag.* NIRMALA *opens it; pours seeds onto her palm.*

Maize. They call it corn in America.

NIRMALA: [*handing it back*] Maize. There are some in the valley who already have this.

LAKSHMI: [*refusing the bag*] Not quite. These have been engineered. Higher yield, for less water. And my client would keep updating your seeds for you, better every time. You wouldn't need to store them anymore.

NIRMALA: Every year before the monsoon, the whole village comes together to share their best seeds. Everything should be for everyone.

LAKSHMI: Perhaps next year you will share these seeds with them.

NIRMALA *looks through the seeds.*

NIRMALA: What else?

LAKSHMI: What?

NIRMALA: What else? There is only one type.

LAKSHMI: Yes, just one crop.

NIRMALA: You came all the way here with just one crop?

LAKSHMI: That's correct.

NIRMALA: But if these fail—

LAKSHMI: They will not fail.

LAKSHMI *gives* NIRMALA *the bottle.*

Mix this with water and spread over the land before planting. Nothing will harm your plants or get in their way. Not bugs, not weeds, excessive moisture or disease. Nothing.

LAKSHMI *gives* NIRMALA *the carton.*

My client's fertiliser. For you to test. Of course, they will provide enough for the full planting if you agree. You will not believe the increase in yield you will achieve. Really, Nirmala. It will stagger you.

LAKSHMI *walks to the edge of their field.*

[*Pointing*] You would need to cut down that clump of trees, and those too, but not much else, for the first planting, just to test, / and see—

ISHA: But our cattle need the trees / for shade—

LAKSHMI: You don't need cow manure if you have that fertiliser.

NIRMALA: But that means—

LAKSHMI: That's right. You wouldn't need the fields you keep to grow their feed. You could change them to maize too, if all goes well. We have plenty of buyers already in place.

NIRMALA: This is madness. Why should we cut down any of our old trees, stop using our cattle, and how could I ever get enough people here to plant at the size you are / saying—

LAKSHMI: Ah. Look.

LAKSHMI *hands* NIRMALA *the envelope.* NIRMALA *opens it.*

That is a cheque. The government will subsidise part of the cost if you plant this much of our maize, and my client will pay the rest as a loan. You will only pay it back when you make a profit.

NIRMALA: A 'cheque'? A 'loan'?

ISHA: It's money, Maa. That is a piece of paper that equals an amount of money. A loan is money you borrow and pay back over time.

NIRMALA: Of course. Money. Money for what?

LAKSHMI: For a tractor, of course. A sizeable one.

ISHA: She doesn't even have a bank account.

LAKSHMI: I will take care of all that for you. I'll guide you through all of this, Nirmala, carefully and slowly.

NIRMALA: A tractor. To work on the land, but not touch it. Ridiculous. No.

She gives back the envelope.

LAKSHMI: Aunty. Why would you keep bending down to the land? Like your husband did?

NIRMALA *points at all the things* LAKSHMI *has tried to give her.*

NIRMALA: I am not a magician. Or a scientist. I do not need your various potions. I am a farmer. And I will feel my land when I work on it.

LAKSHMI *gives her the envelope again.*

LAKSHMI: Get a tractor, woman! Alone, you will do what used to take ten of you to do. You will do it in half a day instead of a week. You, a woman, alone. Will be able to do it. And then Isha … Well.

NIRMALA: [*finally understanding*] … Isha could go back to school. And finish her studies.

LAKSHMI: And be free.

ISHA *and* NIRMALA *look at each other.*

[*To* ISHA] Why science?

ISHA: Sorry?

LAKSHMI: Why do you keep saying that?

ISHA: [*flustered*] What?

LAKSHMI: There is no need to apologise. Why do you want to study science, Isha? Tell me, honestly.

ISHA: … Miss Devi says—

NIRMALA: / Help me, gods—

ISHA: Miss Devi says everyone has their own truth. And science is the process of testing and testing and testing to find out what is most true. She says we can never know everything and sometimes we realise an old truth is not as good as the new one we have discovered and now the new one is the most true, until the day an even better truth comes along … I like that. I want to understand the world. I want to understand the *most true* version of it. I—I *need* to.

LAKSHMI: [*turning to* NIRMALA] Aunty. You wouldn't kill one plant on your farm before it at least had a chance to grow. But you will do this to your own *daughter*?

NIRMALA *thinks.* ISHA *can't believe she hasn't said no yet.*

NIRMALA: What you said before—

LAKSHMI: Yes?

NIRMALA: What does that mean? 'Prodigiously talented'?

LAKSHMI: It means Isha is one of the most intelligent young women Miss Devi has ever met. That I've ever met.

NIRMALA: Is that so?

LAKSHMI: Yes, Aunty.

NIRMALA *mulls on this thought.*

NIRMALA: Hm.

ISHA *starts quietly jumping from foot to foot.*

Be still, Isha!

ISHA *cannot keep still.*

If I do this, child. If I let you go. You must remember. You *are* this place. Your gods are in this forest, and in this river. That will never change.

ISHA: I know, Maa.

NIRMALA: Even in the city, the goddess will still be in you. The river breathes inside of us. I am sure of it.

ISHA *nods, dutiful, quietly simmering with hope.*

[*To* LAKSHMI] You will not go any further into this place. I will test out your potions first. I will see if I can bend it to our ways. If I think they have some use, then, and only then, will I let you come deeper into our valley. Understood?

LAKSHMI: Understood. I will listen to you, Aunty, as much as I will teach. I promise.

NIRMALA *stares at* ISHA. *Then—*

NIRMALA: Okay.

LAKSHMI: Okay?

NIRMALA: Okay, demon. For my daughter. Not for you, you understand? Or for your 'market'. I'm doing this for my daughter.

LAKSHMI: For Isha.

LAKSHMI *turns to* ISHA, *giving her full attention to her.*

Now. I have one more thing to add. If Isha wants it—and this is coming from me, personally, understand? Not my clients. If Isha wants, I will pay for her university education, in Delhi. Or wherever in the world she desires. To become a scientist. To discover the most true version of the world, so she can come back and share it with us. I think that will be a very precious gift for us all.

ISHA: Eeeeeeek!

NIRMALA *is dumbstruck.* ISHA *is doing a happy dance all over the place.*

LAKSHMI: What do you say, Isha? Do you still think I am an idiot?

ISHA *stops dancing. Then, after a moment of consideration, shakes her head.*

NIRMALA: Why? Why would you come here and give us this?

LAKSHMI: Because, Aunty. Every woman in India deserves to be free. And I will not rest until they all are.

ACT TWO

The same setting—seven years later.

NIRMALA *and* DEVI *enter, mid-conversation.* NIRMALA *cuts vegetables as they talk;* DEVI *is writing notes in a little journal. Both have a sense of adrenalin about them—change is in the air.*

DEVI: Let's run the school on the protest site itself—

NIRMALA: Yes, good, Devi. Put the school at the centre of everything. Let the children absorb what is happening around them—

DEVI: Yes! Agreed, Nirmala. I'll do that—

NIRMALA: But the farmers must teach as much as you do—

DEVI: Of course. Are you happy for me to organise that, or—

NIRMALA: Yes. It should be you. You don't speak down to them—

DEVI: Thank you. Okay; so each farmer will come in and share their specialty—

NIRMALA: Yes. Saipriya and potato cultivation. / Meena and her fish traps.

DEVI: Yes, yes. And Didi—

NIRMALA: Yes?

DEVI: Why don't we operate a small farm on the site too? With rotating crops—

NIRMALA: Really?

DEVI: Yes! This way the children can be with their parents at the protest, but still learn everything they would if they were back on their lands.

NIRMALA: Hm.

DEVI: What?

NIRMALA: This way the children will learn what people from other villages have been doing too. They'll grow up knowing more than their parents do.

DEVI: Which is good, no?

NIRMALA: … I think so.

DEVI: Nirmala?

NIRMALA: … Yes. Yes, let's do it, Devi.

DEVI: Good. Good, Didi—

NIRMALA: And the other volunteers? Like you, from the cities?

DEVI: I'll get them to also teach one subject each. To the older kids. Hindi, mass media, / macro-economics—

NIRMALA: Mass? Macro? What are even you talking about, Devi—

DEVI: Like, global media companies. Whole-of-country economics, sometimes multiple countries—

NIRMALA: Chi. Nothing is small anymore, is it?

DEVI: Less and less, Didi.

NIRMALA: And you? Will you teach a specialty too?

DEVI: I'm going to try. To teach them about global development. The UN, the World Bank. These were my old jobs—

NIRMALA: Ah, yes. All the plans the big people have for little people like us, hm?

DEVI: I know. I'm sorry, Nirmala, but—

NIRMALA: Our young ones need to know about that world out there, Devi. I realise that now.

DEVI: I wish it wasn't true. But if they are going to be effective in the struggle—

NIRMALA: How can you fight against something, if you don't know what you are fighting?

DEVI: Exactly.

NIRMALA: Make sure you start and end each school day with ceremony and the struggle songs.

DEVI: Study and struggle go hand in hand.

NIRMALA: [*nodding*] Study and struggle go hand in hand.

DEVI: I'll make sure, Didi.

NIRMALA *reaches out to touch her.*

NIRMALA: I know you will, Devi.

DEVI: Ahem. Even Ranjan is trekking in. He wants to call his class 'making the wild your friend'—

NIRMALA: That boy was supposed to marry Isha, you know.

DEVI: [*suddenly coy*] Oh. Really?

NIRMALA: Ranjan's family never forgave me when I sent her away. She never told you?

DEVI: She didn't talk much about here, when she was in the city. She only wanted to know about our way of things. About everything that was new.

NIRMALA: She has always been that way.

DEVI: I'm not so different.

NIRMALA: You two are nothing alike.

DEVI: Well—

NIRMALA: You, born in the city, with parents who have too much money to know what to do with it, left everything and came here. My own daughter, born onto a land that already gives her everything she needs, left—still wanting more.

DEVI: Didi. You know—in the city—we don't really think about anything but ourselves. Everything—our food, our water—it's just … there. It just *works* for us. But once I started learning *how* it all worked … I knew I had to come here. To learn about a different way. Isha just wanted to learn too. About the parts of the world she didn't know.

NIRMALA: [*suggestive*] You came here just to learn, huh?

DEVI: Sorry?

NIRMALA: I hear Ranjan has found someone new. A love match.

DEVI: [*blushing*] You can't keep a secret in this place.

NIRMALA: A rich city girl, falling in love with the shy wild boy with the chipped tooth? No, you can't hide a secret like that.

DEVI: Anyway—

NIRMALA: [*cajoling*] What, you don't want to talk about it?

DEVI: Okay! / Back to the protest—

NIRMALA: / [*grinning*] Okay, okay! How are we on food for the protestors?

DEVI: Bala came today, with his share of the harvest from his and Saipriya's farm. It'll be enough for us for the week. Next week we'll move onto Ranjan's farm. He's ready.

NIRMALA: Is Bala still grumbling?

DEVI: Yes, still grumbling. Says he saw a tiger this time.

NIRMALA: A tiger?! What an imagination that man has.

DEVI: It grows bolder by the day.

NIRMALA: What did Saipriya say?

DEVI: Saipriya told him she already spoke to this tiger.

NIRMALA: [*laughing*] She did?!

DEVI: [*laughing too*] Bala. [*Impersonating Bala*] You already spoke to her? The tiger?

NIRMALA: And what did this animal say to her?

DEVI: Saipriya said the tigress wants her here. At the *satyagraha*. Protesting. She said if the dams go ahead as the government and the company plan, the rivers the tigers drink from will no longer be fresh; the creatures the tigers like to eat will dwindle in number; not just the birds and mongooses but us humans too. Don't worry husband, she said. This tigress won't hurt you. She is part of the struggle too. The animals are on our side. The river is on our side. That is why we will win.

NIRMALA: She said all that?

DEVI: She did.

NIRMALA: We should keep her here. At the protest. Bala will have to manage.

DEVI: I agree. She wants to stay, Didi. She's eager to learn.

NIRMALA: Very good, Devi. Do you think Saipriya would be comfortable talking to the media? To the government, even?

DEVI: Soon, yes. If I keep teaching her.

NIRMALA: Make sure you focus on her.

DEVI: Okay. I will.

NIRMALA: We'll have to teach her your language.

DEVI: I'll take care of that.

NIRMALA: Isn't it interesting, that Bala never saw a tiger when Saipriya was there to cook and clean for him. He only sees it when he is having to do everything by himself.

DEVI: Very interesting.

NIRMALA: Devi. I'm just—

DEVI: [*gentle*] What?

NIRMALA: This protest. It's—taking people from all the different village groups. Women *and* men. Children. Different castes. And mixing them together. I'm not sure what will happen …

DEVI: People from your part of India and my part of India haven't really worked this way together either, right?

NIRMALA: It's true.

DEVI: It's a great experiment.

NIRMALA: I thought we were joining these protests to protect our way of life. To keep things exactly as they have always been. But actually …

She encounters a new thought.

… the struggle itself is changing us.

DEVI: Is that …

NIRMALA: Devi?

DEVI: Are you okay with that, Nirmala?

NIRMALA: Do I have a choice?

DEVI: 'In the midst of every crisis, lies great opportunity.'

NIRMALA: Who said that?

DEVI: Oh, a famous white scientist.

NIRMALA: Hm. I think that one was right.

DEVI: So do I.

NIRMALA: With crisis, comes many opportunities. Including falling in love with the boy with the chipped tooth.

DEVI: [*blushing*] Didi! Stop it!

NIRMALA: Okay, okay … [*Serious now*] So. How long do we have before the real tigers arrive?

DEVI: It'll be any minute now, Didi.

They look out into the distance.

Will you meet them here? On the riverbank?

NIRMALA: Yes. We will meet here. With the goddess by our side.

DEVI: Will you eat first? / Let me bring you something—

NIRMALA: No, no Devi. You go. Join Saipriya, and the others who are waiting for them, at the head of the river. They need you there. Go, go. I need to think. Come back and tell me when they've arrived.

DEVI: Okay, Didi.

DEVI *embraces* NIRMALA *as a gesture of solidarity.* NIRMALA, *stiff at first, returns the embrace.*

NIRMALA: We will stand up. We will rise.

DEVI: We will stand up. We will rise.

DEVI *leaves.* NIRMALA *walks to the riverbank.*

NIRMALA: Mighty river. Goddess. I need your anger now. Last time the demon came, I was tricked by its kindness. I learnt a valuable lesson that day. I learnt the giving of kindness without the giving of power is no gift at all. I need your fury now. Cover me with it, goddess. Drown me in your fury. And then unleash me.

NIRMALA *begins to growl. Initially, it is calm, controlled. But as it grows it becomes more and more out of control, until it consumes her—*

DEVI *re-enters in a hurry.*

DEVI: Nirmala—

NIRMALA: Yes?

DEVI: They're here. They're on their way.

NIRMALA: They're here? [*Harnessing the strength*] Good. I am ready. Bring them, Devi. / I am ready—

DEVI: No. Nirmala. The—I—

She's tongue-tied.

NIRMALA: What?

DEVI: Two negotiators have arrived—

NIRMALA: Okay—

DEVI: One of them is Lakshmi; / we were expecting her.

NIRMALA: Mmm.

DEVI: She is now one of the leading international environmental consultants working with the multinationals who have to liaise with communities in this part of India.

NIRMALA: What the hell does that mean?

DEVI: It means she is now a tiger with even sharper teeth.

NIRMALA: Okay. Understood. Go on.

DEVI: The other negotiator. She—

She can't speak.

NIRMALA: [*fierce*] Out with it, woman!

DEVI: The other one is Isha.

NIRMALA: … *My* Isha?

DEVI: Yes.

NIRMALA: What is she doing here?

DEVI: Nirmala—they said … they said—

NIRMALA: Yes?

DEVI: They said Isha works for the company now.

NIRMALA: [*stunned*] She *what?*

DEVI: Apparently she is one of their junior scientists.

NIRMALA*'s power dissipates. For a moment, she loses her footing. She looks like she is about to crumble.* DEVI *rushes to help but* NIRMALA *quickly gathers herself.*

Didi—

NIRMALA: No. I'm fine. I'm fine.

She's not fine. DEVI *watches her, concerned.*

DEVI: Um—

NIRMALA: What?

DEVI: How long has it been, since …

NIRMALA: Since what, Devi!

DEVI: Since you've talked to each other?

NIRMALA: Many seasons, Devi. Many. How can we talk? She can't call me here. We do not have phones or computers. To talk to me, she has to come here. And if you live in the city, it takes a long time to do that. Too long, it seems, for her to bother.

DEVI: I'm sure she has her reasons—

NIRMALA: [*gesturing around her*] This is my family now, Devi. The trees, the plants, the villagers, you—you are all my family.

DEVI: I—I'm honoured, Didi. You all belong here. I am just a visitor. But Isha is—

NIRMALA: I was wondering, the other day. I thought, maybe she will never come back. I had that thought.

DEVI: And now she has.

NIRMALA: Yes. Now she has.

Beat.

Why would they bring a junior scientist to the negotiations?

DEVI: Well …

NIRMALA: Devi?

DEVI: [*trying to be delicate*] When you and Isha last talked, did you leave on good terms?

NIRMALA: Yes and no.

DEVI: Yes and no?

NIRMALA: What are you getting at, child?!

DEVI: [*in an outburst*] Maybe they think she will have an influence on you, Nirmala! [*Embarrassed*] Sorry, / I didn't mean to—It's not my place to—

NIRMALA: No, no, you're right, Devi. That is probably what they think, no? … Do you think I should step back from the negotiations?

DEVI: Do *you* think you should?

NIRMALA *considers.*

I could ask Saipriya to—

NIRMALA: I *am* the struggle. I *am* this land. Such things cannot be separated from me, even if my own daughter is trying to convince me otherwise.

DEVI: … Okay, Didi. Okay. Let's still lead the negotiations together. You and I.

NIRMALA: Yes. Good. Good, Devi. We will still do it together.

DEVI: [*gesturing behind her*] So—shall I—

NIRMALA: Yes, bring them here Devi. Let's begin.

DEVI: I will go and get them now.

She leaves. NIRMALA *paces, gathering strength again.*

NIRMALA: Tigress. I am you. River. I am you. Goddess. I am you. Give me strength, for I am you.

ISHA, LAKSHMI *and* DEVI *enter.* ISHA *is now dressed like* LAKSHMI.

ISHA *goes to embrace her mother.*

ISHA: Maa—

NIRMALA *steps back.*

NIRMALA: Isha. We are on either side of a raging river. Is now the right time to try and cross the water?

ISHA: But are we, Maa? Standing on different sides?

NIRMALA: You tell me.

DEVI *is pouring cups of chai.*

NIRMALA: [*curt*] Lakshmi.

LAKSHMI: [*equally curt*] Nirmala.

DEVI: Come! Shall we sit?

They sit. DEVI *gives cups of chai to* LAKSHMI *and* ISHA. NIRMALA *touches* DEVI*'s hand in approval as she passes;* ISHA *sees their closeness.*

ISHA: [*barbed*] Thank you, Miss Devi.

DEVI: I think you can drop the 'Miss' now, Isha.

ISHA: Mmm. You know, I heard you'd left the city, and joined here.

DEVI: Since the day I met you Isha, I've been curious about your homelands—

ISHA: Yes. I've always noticed that about you—

DEVI: It's been an immense privilege to live and help here for these past weeks.

ISHA: A nice little holiday project for you, I suppose.

DEVI: [*defensive*] Isha. That's not—

NIRMALA: Enough.

She looks at LAKSHMI.

Let's begin.

LAKSHMI: Yes, Nirmala. Let's begin.

NIRMALA: The villagers and I have talked. Devi has listened. She knows how you people speak. So she will say to you what we want to say, but in a way that you will understand.

LAKSHMI: Very good, Nirmala.

ISHA: Maa. Devi. We need to—

LAKSHMI: Isha. Let them speak first.

ISHA: But—

LAKSHMI: Isha.

ISHA: … Okay.

LAKSHMI: [*gesturing to* DEVI] Devi.

NIRMALA *paces throughout* DEVI*'s speech, an emotional shadow of her points, making sounds of agreement or disgust as she goes.*

DEVI: For weeks, the villagers across the valley have sat and talked. They have collectively decided their way forward and made a list of demands. Tomorrow, our volunteers will begin travelling to a number of different cities around India, and leave a copy of these demands with each of your board members. We are leaving a copy with the Indian government's environmental department. We will also publish the demands on the internet. Unlike you, everything we do is transparent.

LAKSHMI: Point made. Continue.

DEVI: You must stop building the dams immediately. Set up a process to consult with the local communities here on how they want to manage their lands and their water. Then continue the development, hand in hand with them. We are not anti-development. We are against development without consultation. We are against development of this size and speed. We believe that you are using the *idea* of progress to destroy our way of life, *unnecessarily*.

LAKSHMI: Understood.

DEVI: I will give you only our three key points now.

LAKSHMI: Please.

DEVI *holds up some government documents.*

DEVI: One. There are forests already slated for submergence, *after* the dams have been finished. That is many years away. Yet people are coming in trucks and cutting these forests down now. More trucks came in today! No more trees can be cut down until we have discussed how many and where the dams should go.

LAKSHMI: Mm-hm.

DEVI: Two. Where dam construction has begun, already large deposits of silt are starting to gather upstream of that construction. This makes that land unusable for the villagers' crops. And now people, animals, their cattle, they all get stuck there. Some have died. Mosquitoes are rife. And where are women supposed to bathe? It is cutting off access to the river. People have to walk miles just to access their drinking water. Meanwhile, downstream of the dam construction, the currents are becoming irregular. Villagers can no longer use their log boats to fish. Crocodiles are starting to appear in the waters! There are new problems every day. If the dams go higher and more are built in more sites, the problems will multiply *exponentially*. We have a chance, here and now, to stop all this *before* it spirals out of control.

NIRMALA: / Yes, good Devi—

ISHA: / Lakshmi—

LAKSHMI: Wait, Isha. Go on, Devi. Your last point.

DEVI: Three. You have already begun clearing space in the valley in order to build local offices here for your company. Hundreds of people and dozens of villages have already been displaced. It is not clear where you intend to relocate these people, how much they will be compensated, in what form that compensation will take, or how long the compensation will take to reach them. It is imperative that this be made abundantly clear before you proceed. Furthermore, families are not to be broken up. Every family here has intricate connections with the others and these connections must be maintained if they are moved. People must not, under any circumstances, be moved to the edges of the towns or cities. Already the villagers displaced by the construction of your offices have been offered new jobs cleaning your offices. They are not interested in that way of life. They do not want to join your economy. This is critical.

LAKSHMI: [*looking at* ISHA] I see.

DEVI: These are our key points. The full list of demands will be in the reports we share and publish tomorrow.

NIRMALA: Very good. Good, Devi. [*To* LAKSHMI] You will stop building the dams. Stop, and talk to us first. Okay? Then we will go ahead, together. Okay? Lakshmi? Do you understand?

LAKSHMI: Thank you for that Devi, Nirmala. Let me start by saying, we hear you. I know this process is disruptive for some and we too seek to lessen that disruption to the extent that we can. But I want to be clear, from the outset: we cannot pause on building the dams. I think you know that. An enormous amount of money is already committed to this project, and our current schedule is beholden to those financial partners, including the Indian government, the World Bank, and a number of private partnerships. It has taken a very long time and an extraordinary amount of work just to get to this point; to make the grand dream this government and our company has for this country—to bring good drinking water to the majority of its citizens—become a reality. We will talk to the displaced people about their recovery and rehabilitation from their affected lands. Absolutely. We will try and give them better terms, and good places to move to. Your protest has achieved that already. It is quite a feat. You should be proud. But none of that matters anymore. Not for your particular villages. Not here. Not now.

DEVI: Excuse me?

LAKSHMI: Tell them, Isha.

They all turn to ISHA*; but she is suddenly tongue-tied.*

NIRMALA: Tell us what, Isha?

ISHA: [*to* LAKSHMI] Now?

LAKSHMI: They have spoken. Now it is our turn.

ISHA *takes a deep breath.*

ISHA: Maa. Devi. Foundation construction has begun on a group of dams very close to the villages in this valley.

DEVI: What? No-one has advised us of that—

LAKSHMI: It has begun. Keep going, Isha.

ISHA: … Despite following best practice principles, and working with excellent public and private sector stakeholders, the drilling has had unexpected side effects; pre-existing soil erosion, combined with the particularly bad monsoon season we are having, and other multiplier effects due to global warming, has led to the sand around the site sinking to a level formerly not thought possible in this timeframe. There's now a very high probability of water levels rising; not just at the dam site but far beyond.

NIRMALA: Speak like a human being, Isha. You used to be one.

ISHA: I—Maa. I—

ISHA *is overwhelmed. She can't speak. She gets up and walks away.*

LAKSHMI: Unfortunately, these lands will be flooded soon. You all have to leave. As soon as possible. But we are going to help you. It's going to be okay.

A stunned silence. Then:

NIRMALA: How long do we have?

LAKSHMI: We can't provide exact numbers—

NIRMALA: Isha. How long do we have?

ISHA *pulls herself together. She forces herself to speak.*

ISHA: The best case scenario is one to two months.

DEVI: *What?*

NIRMALA: What is the worst case? Isha?

ISHA: Sometime next week. Maybe the end of this week.

NIRMALA: Are you sure?

ISHA: Maa?

NIRMALA: Are you absolutely certain?

ISHA: We've tripled checked the data and—

NIRMALA: I didn't ask you what everyone else thinks. Or what the data says. I asked if you, you Isha, my daughter, were certain. Is this definitely happening? Our are lands going underwater?

ISHA: … Yes, Maa. Yes. It's definitely happening.

Beat.

NIRMALA: Devi, we need to tell the others. Run to the satyagraha. Tell the protestors first, then tell them to split up and tell the head villagers from each section of this valley. That way everyone will know, soon. Once you've told the protestors, come back, as quickly as possible.

DEVI: Yes, Didi—

She begins to leave.

NIRMALA: And Devi—

DEVI: Yes?

NIRMALA: Tell them that each person gets to decide whether they want to leave, or to stay.

ISHA: No!

NIRMALA: What, Isha?

ISHA: Everyone has to leave—

NIRMALA: It's their choice, Isha. Not yours.

ISHA: [*quietly terrified*] What are *you* going to do?

NIRMALA: I don't know yet.

ISHA: *What?*

NIRMALA: This is my home, Isha. It was yours once too.

ISHA: If you stay, you'll die.

NIRMALA: It's not that simple, / child—

ISHA: / No! Maa—

DEVI: Didi?

NIRMALA: Go, Devi. Go now. And Devi? Don't speak down to them, okay? I know you never do. Just speak clearly and calmly. Tell them I will come to the protest site tonight and we will speak further then and decide our next steps together. But first, make sure everyone knows what has happened. What they have done to us. Go.

DEVI: Okay, Nirmala.

DEVI *goes.* ISHA *moves closer to her mother—*

ISHA: [*pulling out some documents*] Maa. I've drawn up a plan. To get us out of this situation—

NIRMALA: You've made a plan? How kind.

LAKSHMI: Nirmala. Most people out there are not going to stay. You know that. They will want to go. To *live*. Isha has spent every waking hour since she learnt this unfortunate news working on this plan.

I've gotten the company's board—via emergency resolution—to agree to sign off on it if you, as the representative of this valley, agree to it too. I promised them that you will be open to this. But the board have only given me until the end of today. You must agree to this, and you must agree before night falls—

NIRMALA: I'll talk to the others first, and then come back to you.

ISHA: That'll take days!

NIRMALA: And?

ISHA: Please, Maa! This plan, it involves moving this entire set of villages to safe, higher ground—

NIRMALA: 'Moving the villages'? What are we, boxes you just transport from one place to the other?

ISHA: Maa—

NIRMALA: You sound like one of them, Isha! What has happened to you?

LAKSHMI: Nirmala. You *could* hear Isha's plan, or you could let this one go to waste and let the company's risk management team come up with their own plan without your community's involvement. Which would you prefer?

NIRMALA: [*to* LAKSHMI] Fine, devil. [*Turning to* ISHA] Tell me.

ISHA: [*to* LAKSHMI] Thank you. [*To* NIRMALA] Okay. Maa. Firstly, and most importantly, we will keep the families intact, and the relationships between the villagers intact. We will move to another part of the valley where everyone can continue their way of life. The ultimate location will be chosen by the community. All costs will be borne by the company.

NIRMALA: How kind.

ISHA: Secondly, the company will fund a market, / for the long-term, for the larger valley community—

NIRMALA: / Chi—

ISHA: Farmers will be able to sell a portion of their produce to locals from the nearby towns and cities. The company will fund these families with the necessary technology to develop their farms with less labour and for higher yield. / This will—

NIRMALA: / May the gods help us—

ISHA: This will free up more of the girls to go to school, if they so wish—

NIRMALA: We have our own school now, Isha. Here, in the villages. We run it, without any support from that government. And we will decide what the children are taught, / not them, not you—

LAKSHMI: Let her finish, will you!

ISHA: Maa. At no point will the company press any agenda except to develop each family's farm as they themselves choose, / along their own self-determined lines—

NIRMALA: / Ha!

ISHA: I made the company promise that, Maa. It is written into the plan.

NIRMALA: Oh, I'm sure it is.

ISHA: Maa?

NIRMALA: Are you done?

ISHA: … Yes.

NIRMALA: The company this, the company that. Are there any humans at this place? Or do they all hide behind 'the company'?

LAKSHMI: Honestly, Nirmala—

NIRMALA: [*to* LAKSHMI] So you won't pause on building the dams.

LAKSHMI: As I've already said, it's just not logistically possible to do that. We have too many stakeholders with too many varying interests.

NIRMALA: [*to* ISHA] And this idea of relocation to somewhere just like here. Where is that new perfect place, exactly?

ISHA: We'll find it, Maa.

NIRMALA: In the next few days, we'll magically find it, huh?

ISHA: If we could start looking *now*—

NIRMALA: And this plan of yours, where everyone in the village can just pick whatever future they want. It won't work, Isha. It sounds wonderful, but it won't work. Not if *they* are a part of it. Not if *they* control it.

ISHA: *We* will control it—

NIRMALA: If their money makes it possible, they control it, Isha—

ISHA: Now you're just being stubborn for the sake of it—

NIRMALA: I've been down this road before, child! I've been down this road because of *you*. Or have you forgotten already?

ISHA: Maa?

NIRMALA: For you, I let her bring money into this place—

LAKSHMI: Oh, please—

NIRMALA: What?

LAKSHMI: I did everything for you, Nirmala. You could have had everything.

NIRMALA: You did it all for yourself, Lakshmi.

LAKSHMI: Excuse me?

ISHA: Maa. Lakshmi. Please. Can we please just focus here / and talk about my plan—

LAKSHMI: / Just wait, Isha!

NIRMALA: / Quiet, child!

ISHA: Argh!

LAKSHMI: [*to* NIRMALA] I opened up an account for you, I got the government's cheque, I took out a loan for the / remaining costs—

NIRMALA: Yes yes yes. I got your tractor, planted your seeds, used your fertiliser. [*To* ISHA] And she was right; the increase on yield was staggering—

LAKSHMI: I found you good buyers for the maize—

NIRMALA: But apparently, to pay back the loan I needed a bigger harvest. Right?

LAKSHMI: That's how it works, Nirmala!

NIRMALA: It made sense at the time. I sold off most of the cattle. What use were the buggers when I no longer needed their shit? Now it was cheaper to just buy their milk. From a store. Can you believe it?

LAKSHMI: We were scaling up cattle farmers on the other side of the valley—

NIRMALA: So I cleared more land. For *you*, Isha.

ISHA: Maa—

LAKSHMI: I personally underwrote her a bigger loan—

ISHA: Please, can we just get back to—

NIRMALA: / Shut up.

LAKSHMI: / Be quiet.

NIRMALA: I got two more tractors. All of my grazing field was turned into maize. Strangely, I now needed less workers on the farm, not more. That's what they had become—workers. Not the women that I had always laboured and laughed and gossiped with, but my workers. I had to let go of most of them. What to do? They couldn't drive tractors.

LAKSHMI: We offered to teach them, Aunty; they didn't want to learn.

NIRMALA: Why would they? I kept the oldest one only. She was going to die soon anyway. I gave her her own little plot to farm and feed her family on—

LAKSHMI: And I found you other workers—

NIRMALA: Yes. Boys. From in town. To drive the tractors. Do the planting, the harvesting. They would do what they needed to do. Then they would go. Very neat. Simple. Before you knew it, I had paid off the loan.

LAKSHMI: There you were. In the next stage of growth. Ready to scale and make real profit. Everything we had worked so hard for was finally going to come to fruition. Except you couldn't do it, could you, Nirmala?

ISHA: What happened, Maa? Lakshmi told me that you stopped working with her. That you told her to take everything back—

NIRMALA: There were little problems, Isha—

LAKSHMI *snorts.*

Little problems that became little itches in my mind. Some of the weeds were coming back. They were getting used to the pesticides. Lakshmi's company would provide me with new pesticides but every year more weeds would come back. Eventually, the weeds will win, the little itch said. They always do.

LAKSHMI: They haven't won yet, Nirmala—

NIRMALA: The soil was degrading. It was becoming more and more depleted. The little itch spoke to me: it can't go on forever, this system. It is incredible, what it achieves in producing from the land. But this way of farming is a kind of conquering of the soil and eventually it will give up.

LAKSHMI: That day, if it comes, is hundreds of years away—

NIRMALA: But our old system—that system *could* last forever. This one can't, that one can. I couldn't stop thinking about that. Their system: finite. Our system: infinite.

LAKSHMI: You would choose for your people thousands of years of back-breaking pain, over hundreds of years of a more comfortable life? Really, Nirmala?

NIRMALA: I missed Kalu. My favourite bull; and the way he used to bellow whenever I used to rub his belly. You remember, Isha? The way he used to make you giggle and giggle. I would tickle Kalu just to see your face crack open with that smile. I missed that smile.

ISHA: Maa—

NIRMALA: I missed the racket of the pigeons and the storks and the parakeets and the kingfishers. They weren't interested in my fields anymore; we'd cleared most of the trees, diverted the small creeks. When I walked this land, through the fields of maize, it was … silent. *Unnatural.*

LAKSHMI: You were daydreaming. You became irresponsible. All because I helped you have less work to do—

NIRMALA: I started to become disorganised, yes. I was supposed to be doing accounts, and managing the workers, but this was not something I wanted to do. I let it all slip. I think the boys started stealing from me.

LAKSHMI: They did. A lot.

NIRMALA: I don't care.

LAKSHMI: All that we did together. Wasted.

NIRMALA: Then I remembered, Isha! The old woman! That little plot of land! I went back there, to visit her. And there—there, the soil was still *real.* And several birds still came. I started to go there more often, until eventually I just sat there all day. The old woman died, and I still sat there. Everyday. I didn't want to be on my own land anymore. I had grown to hate it. I had grown to hate myself.

ISHA: / Oh, Maa …

NIRMALA: That was when I knew, Isha. I knew I had to give it all back. The tractors, the seeds, the 'market'. You can't bring together the two systems, child. The straight line and the circle. We either do it our way, or their way. There is no middle. That is what I have learnt. Your 'plan'—however well-meaning it is—it won't work. I can't agree to it. I cannot agree to condemn our people to that kind of future.

LAKSHMI: [*to* ISHA] I told you this would happen, Isha. I told you this would be a waste of time—

ISHA: Just—let me speak to her, Lakshmi. Alone.

LAKSHMI: Isha—

ISHA: Please.

LAKSHMI: … Okay.

LAKSHMI *unwillingly steps away and watches from a distance.* ISHA *moves closer to* NIRMALA.

ISHA: You never told me that happened. You never told me you started to hate yourself.

NIRMALA: You haven't been around to tell.

ISHA: Maa—

NIRMALA: Seven harvests, Isha. Seven harvests you've been gone.

ISHA: Has it been that long?

NIRMALA: You don't even know?

ISHA: I—I've been so, so—

NIRMALA: So—what?

ISHA: Busy.

NIRMALA: Busy?

ISHA: Yes!

NIRMALA: Doing what?

ISHA: Working, Maa! Time moves differently in the city—

NIRMALA *starts walking to the river.*

NIRMALA: Seven years, Isha.

ISHA: I wanted to come back. / I just—I couldn't find the right time—

NIRMALA: Mm.

ISHA: What?

NIRMALA: I just—I thought you would have a better reason for your absence, Isha.

ISHA: This place, it's so far away, from everything—

NIRMALA: It is close to itself.

ISHA: It's not close to the rest of the / world, Maa!

NIRMALA: [*soft*] Be quiet, would you.

ISHA: Maa—

NIRMALA: [*suddenly fierce*] Shut up! Just shut up, child!

ISHA, *shocked, says nothing.* NIRMALA *speaks to the river.*

I asked for this, didn't I, goddess? I asked for you to rise—all those years ago, and again, today. I summoned your anger. I knew you would be unstoppable. I asked you to come and kill the demon. Forgive me. I didn't know, goddess. [*Turning to* ISHA] I didn't know, that the demon would be my own child.

ISHA: / Maa!

LAKSHMI: / Nirmala—

NIRMALA: I understand now, goddess. Love is bad. It's a trick. And this—'situation'—is a curse. Your curse. Because I made a mistake. I betrayed you.

ISHA: Would you please stop talking to the water, Maa—

NIRMALA: I should never have let you go, Isha. I only let you go because you were my daughter. Because I loved you. It was a test— [*pointing at the water*] from the goddess— [*pointing at* LAKSHMI] *she* was a test, and we failed. You should have stayed in our village—

ISHA: I would have done anything to leave. You know that.

NIRMALA: You should have stayed.

LAKSHMI: And let her die at sixty?

ISHA: Lakshmi. Let me handle this—

LAKSHMI: [*to* ISHA] No. She needs to hear it. [*To* NIRMALA] Let her get married to someone she didn't want to marry? Working the land instead of exploring and learning the truest version of the world? *Really*, Nirmala? Really?

NIRMALA: Yes, devil. Really.

ISHA: Maa—I was isolated here. I had no choice over who I would spend my time with or what I would grow up to do. I wanted to get out. You *helped* me get out—

NIRMALA: I get it, Isha. I really do. I was born in a mud house in this place, like every woman for tens of thousands of years before me. And in one generation, my daughter is the first person in our village to go to university. She is now a scientist in one of the biggest companies in the world. I get it.

LAKSHMI: Exactly. Progress.

NIRMALA: Yes. Your 'progress'. But—

LAKSHMI: But what?

NIRMALA: For this 'progress' to happen, my daughter must live so far away she can no longer see me. Isn't there something very basically wrong about that? This 'progress'. That means we must—break up our families. We must uproot them from their lands. Where they have always been. Where they belong—

LAKSHMI: No-one forced you to send Isha away. You made a choice. A good choice—

NIRMALA: And yet I don't feel like I made a choice. I feel like I was tricked.

LAKSHMI: You always have a choice.

NIRMALA: Now, too late, I get it. Better to change the problems of where we are, whatever they are, no? That is what our protests are doing, no? Rather than just run away to new places and new problems. This is what I am thinking now. This is the new itch in my mind. I should never have let my daughter go.

LAKSHMI: You let Isha go because the problems here felt *immune* to change. Because she was hungry. Hungry for a better life!

ISHA: I wanted to go, Maa! I was desperate for it. / Bloody hell—

NIRMALA: Love is a trick, don't you see? You were a test, Lakshmi, sent by the gods, and I failed—

ISHA*'s had enough.*

ISHA: You were impossible to live with! Okay?!

NIRMALA: [*soft*] What?

ISHA: That's why I left! Because you were impossible to live with! I couldn't breathe, you mad woman. I couldn't do anything that was my own choice. I couldn't be myself! That's why I never came back, Maa. I couldn't—I was still so—Grrrr. I was still so *angry* with you. Even after all these years, I was still so—angry. I didn't want to come back. And just start fighting / with you again—

NIRMALA: We failed the test, Isha! And the goddess has cursed us.

ISHA: Oh please! She doesn't even exist.

NIRMALA: *What?*

ISHA: Your gods—all of these gods—they don't exist.

NIRMALA: Is that so?

ISHA: They're just a lie, Maa. A nice lie we had to make up for ourselves before we were able to learn the real truth of the world.

NIRMALA *picks up her scythe.*

NIRMALA: Demon.

LAKSHMI: Nirmala—

NIRMALA: Seven years. Okay. Fine. Don't come back. If you don't like it here, don't come back. Fine.

ISHA: Maa—

NIRMALA: But *why*, Isha? Why on earth would you join *them*? Why would you go and *work* for that idiot?

LAKSHMI: C'mon, Aunty—

ISHA: Lakshmi brought me on to *change* the way they work. If I can change that company, then I change the future of millions of people like us. Isn't that worth trying, Maa?

NIRMALA: Demon.

NIRMALA *advances on* ISHA.

LAKSHMI: Nirmala. Think rationally.

NIRMALA: When Lakshmi told you they were flooding our village, why didn't you pick up a sword and just cut her off at her legs? Why didn't you march upstairs to all those bosses and cut off all of their heads?

ISHA: Maa. What happened was out of their control. They didn't *want* this to happen—

NIRMALA: When you work with the devil, you become like them. It is inevitable, Isha. How stupid I was, to let you go. So bloody stupid. I see now what I have to do.

ISHA *finds another sharp tool and picks it up. They are circling each other now.*

ISHA: No. No more, Maa. No more.

NIRMALA: Love is a curse, Isha. And I must lift this curse from our home.

ISHA: Listen to me! Listen to me, you intractable old woman. I'm the one who has been out there. I'm the one who understands how our world is changing. We have to change with it. Otherwise it will come and consume us. It is coming *now*. You hear me? *Now.*

NIRMALA: Exactly, Isha. Don't you see? You haven't stopped believing. You simply believe in a different god now. A god that consumes, endlessly. That is who you pray to now, no? But listen, child. You have been deceived. Run away from your new god one day and it will still find a way to hunt us down the next. Pray to this new god, and there is no escape, Isha. It only knows how to eat you.

NIRMALA *raises her scythe.* ISHA *raises hers in self-defence.* LAKSHMI *moves to protect* ISHA *with her own body—*

LAKSHMI: / Nirmala! Stop this madness!

ISHA: / Maa!

NIRMALA *screams and attacks* ISHA *with her scythe.* ISHA *and* LAKSHMI *defend themselves, screaming.* DEVI *re-enters in a rush.*

DEVI: Didi! What are you doing?!

DEVI *tackles* NIRMALA *to the floor, physically moving her away from* ISHA *and* LAKSHMI.

NIRMALA: I need to lift the curse. / It's all my fault—I let her go—

She repeats several times.

DEVI: It won't change a thing, Nirmala! Hurting them. I get it! Truly. But it won't change a thing!

They sit, out of breath, on the floor.

NIRMALA: You're right. A curse is a curse. It cannot be lifted, just like that. [*Muttering to herself*] / You're right. You're right. It won't change a thing.

DEVI: Not like this. Not like this, Didi. Not like this.

NIRMALA *drops her scythe.*

LAKSHMI: For god's sake, Nirmala. Will you please just sign these papers now? And agree to the plan that Isha and I have worked tirelessly, day and night, to get over the line for you?

ISHA: Maa? Will you?

NIRMALA *turns to* DEVI.

NIRMALA: Did you tell the others?

DEVI: I told everyone gathered at the protest. They've split up to tell the others. All of the village heads are coming here, now. We will talk soon, together.

NIRMALA: Good.

DEVI: And Didi—

NIRMALA: Yes?

DEVI: Most want to leave. But many want to stay, too.

NIRMALA: They do?

DEVI: Mm-hm. In fact, Saipriya says there is no need to stop the protest. We should still continue, no? Even if we drown. Saipriya says, *this* should be our new demand. We will stay, and we will drown. Unless you stop building the dam. Ranjan agreed with her. Many others did too. They want to stay. And they think they will have the blessings of their families to do so.

NIRMALA: They want to stay?

DEVI: It is their right, no?

NIRMALA: I see.

NIRMALA *stands, and locks eyes with* ISHA.

ISHA: [*quietly terrified*] Maa?

NIRMALA: I see now what I must do. To lift the curse.

ISHA: [*softly now*] No, Maa …

NIRMALA: I'm going to stay, Isha. I must stay. That is my punishment. For letting you go—

ISHA: Maa. No-one can stay. Please. I came here to help you all *live*—

NIRMALA: Each can make their own choice. [*To* LAKSHMI] There is always a choice, no?

ISHA: Please. Take my plan instead. Please, Maa—

NIRMALA: [*softly too*] Isha. If you don't want me to die, figure out a way to stop our lands from being flooded. Okay? [*Turning to* DEVI] This is our new demand, yes? Our only one now.

DEVI: [*holding* NIRMALA*'s wrist*] Yes—Yes, this will be our new demand. We will stay, and we will drown, unless you stop the construction.

NIRMALA: You want to stay too, Devi?

DEVI: If you will let me.

ISHA: This is so stupid.

DEVI: I am not here on a holiday.

NIRMALA: I know you aren't, Devi.

DEVI: I will send this new message to the media tomorrow. No pausing on the construction, no working hand in hand with the company. Just stop it. Stop it, and leave us forever, or we will drown.

NIRMALA: Good. Simple. Much clearer.

ISHA *and* LAKSHMI *look at each other.*

LAKSHMI: Do you want to tell them, or should I?

NIRMALA: Tell us what?

ISHA: [*turning to* NIRMALA] Maa. Please listen to me. People will come. If you do this.

NIRMALA: People?

ISHA: Maybe the army. Maybe thugs. That was always the company's back up plan. If you didn't accept mine.

NIRMALA: Lakshmi knew already? That some of us would want to stay?

ISHA *shakes her head.*

ISHA: … But I did.

NIRMALA: … And you *told* her?

ISHA: [*broken now*] … I wanted to keep you alive.

LAKSHMI: Isha's right. The government will bring the police in. The army, if necessary. I've already discussed it with them.

NIRMALA: To do what?

LAKSHMI: To move you. Peacefully, of course. But once you're in their hands, we're not responsible for what happens to you. Where you get moved to. What compensation you are eligible for anymore. You may even be tried in court. Alternatively—you could just sign Isha's plan.

NIRMALA: On what charge would they put us in court?

LAKSHMI: You are disrupting an approved construction project with an illegal protest, Nirmala.

NIRMALA: But why would they bother doing that? Won't they let us die in peace?

DEVI: What she is saying is, if no-one knows you are dying, then it's okay. Tell the media you're dying, then they'll move you.

ISHA: That's not / what she's saying—

DEVI: / Essentially, it is—

NIRMALA: / [*to* LAKSHMI] Wait. How do you know this will happen?

ISHA: No, she's saying that if you go to the media then this will start to get out of hand and we won't be able to do the plan / I've sorted out with the company—

NIRMALA: Shut up! Everyone! Lakshmi. How do you know, really? That the police will come?

ISHA: She's got the Prime Minister on speed dial, Maa—

NIRMALA: [*to* LAKSHMI] But—why? Why *would* they come? To our little village? That's 'far away from everything'?

LAKSHMI: What are you saying, Nirmala? Spit it out.

NIRMALA: You're bluffing.

LAKSHMI: God, you're infuriating.

NIRMALA: They're bluffing, Devi.

LAKSHMI: I've had enough of this. / Let's go, Isha—

ISHA: No. We can't go, Lakshmi! We can't leave them / like this—

NIRMALA: Why would the police come all the way here, to stop our little protest? It will take them days. How many are they going to send, anyway? To this far-off place. Some small number. We can resist them, no? Tie ourselves to the earth, somehow—

DEVI: Maybe you're right, Didi—I'm not sure—

NIRMALA: I'm not scared of a few idiotic men. We will fight them off, no?

LAKSHMI: This is ridiculous. Come, Isha. Let's go—

ISHA: [*to* LAKSHMI] Wait. They are coming, right? You're not bluffing?

LAKSHMI: Yes, Isha. They're coming.

ISHA: But how *do* you know?

LAKSHMI: Isha—

ISHA: This is such a far-away place. If some of the villagers stay, will police really come, to move them to safety? Or will they just be allowed to drown?

LAKSHMI: They'll come. The police.

NIRMALA: How do you know?

LAKSHMI *shakes her head.*

ISHA: Tell us, Lakshmi!

LAKSHMI: … It's what they've done already. In other places.

NIRMALA: / What other places?

ISHA: / There are other places?

LAKSHMI: Never mind.

DEVI: How many other places?

LAKSHMI: I don't know.

DEVI: Yes, you bloody well do.

LAKSHMI: No. I'm not going to—

ISHA: Lakshmi. There are other places? That are going to be flooded? That have already been flooded? What are you talking about?

NIRMALA: [*to* ISHA] You don't know?

ISHA: I'm working on a certain number of villages. The ones that have been allocated to me. Not all of them. The dam construction is too big for anyone to be across all of it.

She turns to LAKSHMI.

I thought our village was the only one that was going to be flooded—

LAKSHMI: Isha—

ISHA: How many, Lakshmi? Where? When?

LAKSHMI: The only reason we even came here is because I wanted to help you. We tried. It didn't work, okay? Now let's go back home—

ISHA: Tell us! Now. Or I will go to the media myself.

NIRMALA *and* DEVI *turn to* ISHA, *surprised.*

LAKSHMI: And tell them what?

ISHA: That, that—that even if the villagers stay here, you will continue building the dams near here, even if they will drown. That, that—even their possible deaths won't stop you building—

LAKSHMI: That would be very stupid, Isha. For all of us.

NIRMALA: You are flooding our homelands. The least you can do is tell us the truth.

LAKSHMI: We are not doing the flooding. It is due to factors outside of our control—

DEVI: [*furious*] Factors outside of your control? Is that what she's been saying?

ISHA: [*to* DEVI] Sorry?

DEVI: [*to* ISHA] They knew exactly what they were doing.

ISHA: What?

LAKSHMI: It was never our plan for something like this to happen—

DEVI: Bullshit. You knew. I've worked with companies like yours before. You know that every big thing you build will have some unintended consequences for someone. You factor that into your modelling, no? The bosses get bonuses if less people are killed. Or what do you call it? 'Affected.' That's why I left all that, to become a teacher. I couldn't stomach that part. That CEOs would get a bigger bonus, if less people died—

NIRMALA: [*to* LAKSHMI] Did you know? That our lands would be flooded regardless, before you started this project?

LAKSHMI: I don't have time for all of this.

ISHA: Did you know, Lakshmi?

LAKSHMI: Aunty. Just sign off on Isha's plan. Please. Or I'm leaving—

NIRMALA: DID YOU KNOW, DEMON?!

ISHA: [*on edge*] Lakshmi. Just tell us. Did you?

LAKSHMI: Isha. You already know the answer.

ISHA: No, I don't.

LAKSHMI: Yes, you do. It's always been there, if you were brave enough to look.

NIRMALA: Tell us!

LAKSHMI: … Of course I knew.

They are stunned.

ISHA: … How many places?

LAKSHMI: Enough of this now.

ISHA: How many places is the company—are we—doing this to? On *purpose*?

LAKSHMI: Enough. [*To* NIRMALA] I came to tell you as soon as I could, as a favour to Isha. I got Isha's plan approved by my leadership, even though they all fought against it, as a favour to her. I have moved heaven and earth for that daughter of yours. Because she is brilliant. *She is brilliant!* And brilliant women deserve every opportunity we can bend the world to give them. After all this time, Isha feels like a daughter to me, too. So I did this for her. You can still live, if you choose to, Nirmala. But I've done all I can. Come, Isha. I'm sorry, but your mother won't sign. You tried, okay? You—we—really tried.

LAKSHMI *goes to leave.* ISHA *doesn't move—*

NIRMALA: Tie her up.

LAKSHMI: Excuse me?

NIRMALA: You haven't answered all our questions. Answer them, or we'll tie you up.

LAKSHMI: You'll be put in prison.

NIRMALA: By who? There are no cameras here. No police. Not yet. There's only us. Devi, tie her up.

LAKSHMI: You can't be serious.

DEVI *grabs* LAKSHMI *and begins to tie her hands up with her scarf.* LAKSHMI *resists.*

Get off me! Isha, get her off me!

NIRMALA *joins to help* DEVI. *She trips* LAKSHMI*'s legs so she falls on the floor—*

[*Still resisting*] Isha, tell them to stop.

ISHA *watches them, considering.*

Isha! Stop them!

ISHA *walks over and helps them tie* LAKSHMI *up. Together, the three of them are able to combat* LAKSHMI*'s fierceness.*

Isha …

ISHA: I want to know.

LAKSHMI: What?

ISHA: I want to know. The truest version of this world. You've been hiding it from me. All this time, you've been hiding it from me.

LAKSHMI *is tied up now.*

NIRMALA: So. Tell us. How many places are going to be flooded?

LAKSHMI *says nothing.*

ISHA: Tell us!

LAKSHMI: Do you really want to know?

ISHA: Yes.

LAKSHMI: [*to* NIRMALA] And then you'll untie me?

NIRMALA: Yes.

LAKSHMI: Fine. Okay. From this set of dams? In your part of the valley? Or all of them?

ISHA: We'll start with this set of dams.

LAKSHMI: And over how long?

NIRMALA: What?

LAKSHMI: These are huge projects. They take decades to complete—

ISHA: Let's say—over the next ten years.

LAKSHMI: Fine. From this set of dams, all along this river … About forty thousand families in about two hundred and twenty sites are going to be flooded.

DEVI: So … around two hundred thousand people?

LAKSHMI: Around that, yes.

Stunned silence.

NIRMALA: And none of these people know that their homes are going to be submerged? That their forests are going to be submerged? That their river, their goddess, is going to turn on them without warning, their source of faith and hope and security is going to become the devil herself, swallowing them whole?

LAKSHMI: I do not believe that any of these people know that their water levels will rise, and by how much, no.

More silence, as they take it in.

ISHA: And all of the dams?

LAKSHMI: That we are building? In India? Or globally?

ISHA: Oh my god. Just in India, for now.

LAKSHMI: Just the ones we are involved in, or everything we know the Indian government to have been building or developing?

DEVI: Everything India is building.

LAKSHMI: On current estimations … Somewhere between thirty and fifty million people.

ISHA: Thirty and fifty million people—displaced? From their homelands?

LAKSHMI: Yes.

More silence.

ISHA *walks up to* LAKSHMI *and slaps her.*

ISHA: Fuck you.

LAKSHMI: Oh, please Isha. You're better than that.

NIRMALA: The 'plan' Isha is offering us. I imagine these other people are not given such a plan.

LAKSHMI: No-one is given that kind of plan. I told you. I was doing this as a favour, to Isha.

NIRMALA: And what about everyone else? What happens to the thirty to fifty million people who don't have a daughter working for the company working with the government to do this?

LAKSHMI: Nirmala—

NIRMALA: What happens to them, Lakshmi?

DEVI: It will be as if they never existed.

Pause.

ISHA: Unless we tell everyone about it. If the people in the cities knew, they would never accept this—

LAKSHMI: Tell them what, Isha? You think this is some big secret no-one knows about?

ISHA: They don't know the *extent* of it—

LAKSHMI: C'mon, Isha! Think! You're better than this!

You forget. I understand life here, along this river. Yes? I told you. That was my grandparents' life. It was horrendous. Nature is horrendous, Isha! Its sun and its storms, its weeds and its dirt, its tigers and its mosquitoes. All of it, out to hurt us. To beat us down.

Then us humans. We figured it out. We figured out how to control nature. How to protect ourselves from it, to use it for *our* needs. And why wouldn't we? The damn thing was going to destroy us if we weren't going to get to it first.

But we weren't allowed into the club, Isha! For hundreds of years the West stole from us, to beat back nature. Those motherfuckers took our resources and used our labour and our land to build up *their* cities in *their* countries. They made us their slaves and servants and killed us if we tried to resist.

But they are not getting away with that bullshit anymore. We have risen up and demanded our fair share. We are the *majority*, no? There are more of us than them. And we deserve progress too. We have told them; you can no longer keep it from us. Now it is *our* time. Now *we* will rise.

The dams that are being built along this river are displacing forty thousand families in order to give drinking water to forty million people in the cities. If that is what has to be done, then that is what has to be done.

Soon, the West will be forgotten. They will be sitting at the back. We are in the front. It is *our* time now. You can't stop it. No-one will want you to stop it. We do not go backwards. Only forwards. Only forwards.

Of course they know already! The people in the cities. Deep down, they all know. Everything comes at a cost, and ultimately, we are comfortable with that cost. You can tell everyone about this if you like. Go on. And many people—many, many people—will *pretend* to be upset about it. But they won't be willing to sacrifice their comfort. Once you have it, you will do *anything* to keep it.

She turns her full attention on ISHA.

And *you.* Oh, you knew Isha. You're a smart person. A brilliant person. At any point you could have asked me more questions. If you knew this was happening here, why didn't you ask if it was happening elsewhere? But you *didn't*, did you? You were too scared to face the answer. But you knew.

The only difference between me and you, between me and all the others in the city like you, is that I do not hide my true intentions. I know that for something to be gained, something else must be lost. You know it too, you are just too scared of being shamed to say it out loud. Say it! Say it! We are the lucky ones, and our luck has only come about at the cost of others. They are welcome to have what we have, but only if we do not have to lose a thing. Not a single thing.

ISHA *is shattered.*

DEVI *snorts.*

What, woman?

DEVI: For something to be gained, something must be lost. Exactly.

NIRMALA: Devi?

DEVI: It's a fantasy. A charade. The whole thing is not possible. It was never possible.

LAKSHMI: What are you on about?

DEVI: This 'progress.' It was never for us.

LAKSHMI: It can be. And it will be. If idiots like you don't mess it up.

DEVI: If, say, tomorrow, everyone in Asia began to consume as much as people in the West do, the planet would be stripped bare. There would be nothing left within a matter of months. Your 'progress' would be over. We can't all have what the West has, Lakshmi. In fact, it was *always* the plan that the West would have it, and we would not. This planet, it has limits. Its resources are not infinite, as much as your imagination is.

LAKSHMI: We will find a way. We will invent the technologies to make it possible. We always do. Science, yes, Isha? Humans will always find a way. To keep growing. To keep progressing.

DEVI: And these new technologies. What will go into them? What minerals? What chemicals? Where will *those* be found? Who will be the next wave of people to be disappeared for the next wave of progress? The new problem requires a new solution which creates new problems which requires new solutions and so it goes on forever! I am sick to death of this system which requires one community to be destroyed for another to benefit.

LAKSHMI: There is no other way. It's how the world works.

NIRMALA: No. That's the opposite of the way this world works, Lakshmi. Nature does not beat us down. You've got it backwards. The limits nature sets for us are limits we are supposed to *mimic*. It's the goddess' way of trying to help us.

She gestures offstage.

Look at this *tendu*. It never grows bigger than it should. Sometimes it is a plant, sometimes a tree, depending on the size of the place it is in. But either way, it is perfect. It contributes to this place—providing fruit, pollen, shade, oxygen. When it dies, it preserves itself by becoming part of the soil that grows the next plant after it. Limits are good, you know. Freedom is more dangerous than you think. I didn't need to send you out, Isha, to learn. We had the most true version of the world here, already. Under our eyes. Under this little tree. The land is more powerful than money will ever be.

LAKSHMI: No. It isn't.

NIRMALA: Yes, it is. Nature is real. Money is an invention.

LAKSHMI: I agree Nirmala, I agree. But in this world, what's real is nothing compared to a beautiful invention. Nature kills us. Money frees us. That is the genius of humans. We will *invent* a way to prosper in this world, even when it is trying to murder us. We make our own myths now. We are the gods now, walking on this earth. We are in control of our own destiny. We have inherited the earth indeed. Life is nothing but a story, it's just that some don't know it, and others actually act upon it. I *refuse* to be a victim. You are all in love with it.

NIRMALA: Oh, Lakshmi. You are a god, I agree. But they have played a trick on you, your godly friends. Because before you came to the earth, they made you a devil, and you don't know it. You are a warning to the rest of us—*be careful or you will all die*. It's the oldest story in the world, don't you know? It has more power than your new ones. The goddess gave us this earth on one condition—*don't destroy it*. They asked us one thing, one thing only, and we couldn't do it. And now you have shown me, that the destruction is so much more than I could imagine it to be. It is so complete. So the gods sent down one final warning—and that is you, Lakshmi—you are the warning of our doom. And maybe I will be the first ghost, but you will be the last. And you will still be a ghost. You will still be a ghost. And you will die blind, Lakshmi, deceived by your own kind. A messenger unaware of her own message. A masked performer with nothing underneath to hide. For if you are a god, the gods have become empty. Nameless Placeless Anythings. And what are we if we pray to emptiness? Where are we if we pray to anywhere? Who are we if we pray to no name? No. That is not for me, woman. For my stories are not inventions. They are stories of the sun and the water and the earth. They are as real as the earth's warmth and its cold and its soil. I will die, but my gods never will. They never will. They never will.

LAKSHMI: You cannot change, that is all. You are rock. You are concrete. You refuse to bend, even when it benefits you. [*To* ISHA] I told you she would be like this. I warned you.

ISHA: … You did.

LAKSHMI: [*to* NIRMALA] Now untie me. I told you what you wanted to know. [*To* ISHA] And let's get the hell out of this god-forsaken valley.

No-one moves.

Then:

DEVI: [*pointing at* LAKSHMI] We should leave her here. Let her die if the waters rise. It would only be fair.

NIRMALA: Make her the sacrifice? If they do not stop the dams?

DEVI: Yes. Exactly. [*To* ISHA] If her own life is on the line, she'll find a way to stop the dams.

LAKSHMI: You idiots. The police will come and throw you all in prison—

NIRMALA: Who's going to tell them, Lakshmi?

LAKSHMI: If I don't come back, they'll send out people to look for me—

ISHA: You would, wouldn't you?

LAKSHMI: What?

ISHA: Find a way to stop it. If it was your own life you were going to lose.

LAKSHMI: We do not go backwards. Only forwards. Only forwards. Only for—

DEVI *goes to put a shawl around* LAKSHMI*'s mouth, so she can't talk.*

Hey. Hey—HEY! ISHA!

Muffled screams from LAKSHMI.

ISHA: [*coldly*] You should conserve your energy, Lakshmi. While we decide what to do with you.

LAKSHMI *fumes, but stops trying to speak.*

NIRMALA *paces, quiet, turning over what to do next. She goes up to* DEVI *first.*

NIRMALA: I'm sorry.

DEVI: Didi?

NIRMALA: I told you Isha would not affect me. Or the negotiations. But she did. Love is a trick. A curse.

She seems lost.

And it keeps tricking me, even now—

ISHA: Maa—

NIRMALA: Wait, Isha. [*To* DEVI] I wanted to say that to you. That is all. That I'm sorry. Before you go.

DEVI: Go, Nirmala? Go where?

NIRMALA: Devi, you cannot stay with us.

DEVI: Didi. I want to—

NIRMALA: No, Devi. I have another path for you.

DEVI: … You do?

NIRMALA: Go throughout the valley—and tell everyone about this. Everything Lakshmi has told us. Spread the news. Of the water rising. The floods that are coming. Disperse the people of our village into the other villages. I'm sure the others will be happy to take them in. Tell the media that some of us are staying, and we will drown if they continue building the dams, and we are prepared for that. But that is not your path. You need to continue the protests. You need to keep the struggle alive. You need to spread it, across the whole region.

DEVI: But … how can we do it without you?

NIRMALA: Everything I know, I learnt from those before me. Knowledge only exists to pass it on, no?

DEVI *slowly realises this is a goodbye.*

DEVI: Yes …

NIRMALA: Saipriya will lead. You will support her. Take Ranjan with you too. Yes?

DEVI: … Yes. Okay.

NIRMALA: Good. Now go. Go, Devi. Okay?

They embrace.

DEVI: It's all we have, Didi.

NIRMALA: What?

DEVI: It's all we have. Stupid, painful, miserable love. It's all we have. Is that a blessing, or a curse? I don't know …

NIRMALA: Devi—

DEVI: Maybe you can love your daughter again, Nirmala. Not as her protector, but as her … collaborator. She is your daughter, yes. But she is also her own woman now.

NIRMALA *turns to look at* ISHA, *trying to summon fresh eyes with which to look.*

Bye, Isha.

ISHA: Bye, Miss Devi.

DEVI: Goodbye, Didi.

NIRMALA: Goodbye, Devi.

DEVI *leaves.*

She's right.

NIRMALA *shrugs.*

She's right. But that doesn't make it any easier.

ISHA: You were right.

NIRMALA: Hm?

ISHA: I should never have left, Maa.

NIRMALA: [*surprised*] Isha—

ISHA: I wanted to be free, so badly. As if such a thing exists. I walked out of your prison and straight into another one.

She looks at LAKSHMI.

NIRMALA: Isha. I am glad you left.

ISHA: [*stunned*] What?

NIRMALA *sighs, then stands. She picks up the scythe.*

LAKSHMI *is terrified as* NIRMALA *advances upon her.*

NIRMALA *pulls* LAKSHMI*'s hands towards her—and cuts the shawl.*

NIRMALA *and* ISHA *watch as* LAKSHMI *unties herself fully.*

LAKSHMI *stands and holds her head up high—no shame.*

LAKSHMI: [*to* ISHA] Are you coming?

ISHA: … No.

LAKSHMI: [*disappointed*] Suit yourself.

ISHA *watches* LAKSHMI *go.* NIRMALA *walks away from them, to the edge of her field. She gestures offstage.*

NIRMALA: Remember?

ISHA: … The paintings.

NIRMALA: Yes. The paintings.

ISHA: Maa—We have to find someone to take those rocks to a new site, / we can't leave them here—

NIRMALA: Isha. Those paintings are of this place. That is their power. They can never be moved, you understand?

ISHA *takes this in, then nods.*

Do you remember the face?

ISHA: Of course. The human face.

NIRMALA: Makes you wonder, no? That we humans were drawing ourselves all that time ago.

ISHA: Fifty thousand years ago—

NIRMALA: Were they drawing a goddess?

ISHA: Or themselves?

NIRMALA: Or both?

ISHA *nods, a new thought dawning on her.*

ISHA: Fifty thousand years. That's reality.

NIRMALA: Isha?

ISHA: Not what's out there, in the cities. Out there is a few hundred years. And it's built on a whole lot of inventions that can't last. That won't last. Parts of it are so incredible, Maa, but overall it's a … performance. That's all. A performance that has to end, at some point. That world out there, right now? It won't last another thousand years, if they keep going the way they're going. The whole thing is a mirage. Here? This? This soil. Our forests. This air. This is it. This is the real world, isn't it?

NIRMALA *smiles, and holds* ISHA*'s face.*

NIRMALA: Yes, darling. And we've been taking care of it. We're taking care of it until they come to their senses, even if that doesn't happen until our grandchildren or beyond. That's my job, Isha. To keep *this* all alive until *that* time comes. When we finally see the real world for what it is again.

ISHA: Your gods—our gods. They're real. They're all around us.

NIRMALA: Yes. But they have no power anymore.

ISHA: Maa?

NIRMALA: The only reason you were able to tell us about the river rising is because you went away. If you hadn't left, we would know nothing. The rivers would have just risen and we would have drowned.

ISHA: [*hopeful*] And now? Will you choose to live?

NIRMALA: Your path, Isha … It was never to be free. It was to learn. To always learn, to keep learning. About that new power. That Lakshmi holds, and everyone like her. They have the power. I see that now. They have the technology. It is incredible. But they've chosen the wrong gods. All that power. It is in service of the wrong gods. And it's your duty to tell them. To convince the people in the city to bend their power towards our gods.

ISHA: [*realising*] … You want me to go back. To the city.

NIRMALA: Yes.

ISHA: Will you come with me?

NIRMALA: Isha—

ISHA: Please. People will listen to you. I'm just some girl—

NIRMALA: I can't leave here, Isha. You knew that, before you even came back here. No?

ISHA: Then I'm staying also.

NIRMALA: I want that, darling. So much. But you can't. Because now your land will be gone. It will be drowned.

ISHA: [*overwhelmed*] Yes.

NIRMALA: And when your land is gone, you will die too.

ISHA: What?

NIRMALA: The old Isha. The person you used to be. She will die too. She cannot exist anymore, if this place no longer does.

ISHA: But then what will happen to me?

NIRMALA: You will rise again, child. The question is, who will the next Isha be?

ISHA: … I can't do it.

NIRMALA: They need you, darling. They need you more than I need you.

ISHA: I can't.

NIRMALA: It was seven years ago. That I told you.

ISHA: Hm?

NIRMALA: Before you left. What did I say?

ISHA: [*remembering*] … That, wherever I go, the goddess will still be in me. The river breathes inside of us, too.

NIRMALA: Which means I will be in you also. Always.

ISHA *looks to her mother.*

ISHA: … Okay.

NIRMALA: Okay?

ISHA *nods.*

ISHA: Okay. I'll do it.

NIRMALA *holds* ISHA*'s hand in thanks.*

NIRMALA: Tonight, I will meet with the others at the protest site. And we will decide our next steps. And we will let you know.

ISHA: Good, Maa.

NIRMALA: … You know what I'm going to do tomorrow?

NIRMALA *murmurs sympathetically to what* ISHA *says below.*

ISHA: Oh, you're probably going to bathe in the river and pray to her. Then you're going to work the land, talking to the parakeets and the kingfishers as you go. You will eat what you and the village have grown. And you will sleep with the valley's wind cooling your tired body.

NIRMALA: One day you'll understand, Isha. Days like that are as good as it gets. What I do, everyday? It's already enough. One day, when we see that the few only ever want more, and we, the many, already have enough—on that day, the world will change.

Finally, they embrace.

ISHA: Bye, Maa.

NIRMALA: Bye, Isha. Tell them, Isha. Tell them about our gods. Go, go. Go.

ISHA *leaves.*

NIRMALA *looks to the river.*

Was it always going to be this way, goddess? A long time, ago, when she was still a kid, Isha told me about that … what was it? Evolution. Those fish. Not content with the ocean. With their rivers. With you. They had to see what was beyond. They weren't made for the land but they found a way to survive on it. As soon as that first fish started breathing from the air, was it always going to be this way? Were we destined to always be aching for more? To be forever hungry? … I don't know. Only you do. Or maybe, you don't either? Is that the great experiment, then? To see which way we will choose? … It's too big a question for me, goddess. I'm going to leave that one with you. I have a river to bathe in, and a place to take care of.

She exits, singing to the goddess as she goes.

THE END

www.ingramcontent.com/pod-product-compliance
Lightning Source LLC
Chambersburg PA
CBHW050023090426
42734CB00021B/3401

* 9 7 8 1 7 6 0 6 2 9 5 9 5 *